I0606158

LOVE POEMS

Also by Rupi Kaur

milk and honey

the sun and her flowers

home body

healing through words

milk and honey: 10th Anniversary Collector's Edition

LOVE POEMS

RUPI KAUR

Andrews McMeel
PUBLISHING®

Love Poems copyright © 2026 by Rupi Kaur. All rights reserved.
Printed in the United States of America. No part of this book may be used or reproduced in any manner whatsoever without written permission, except in the case of reprints in the context of reviews.

The authorised representative in the EEA is Simon and Schuster Netherlands BV, Herculesplein 96 3584 AA Utrecht, Netherlands. (info@simonandschuster.nl)

Andrews McMeel Publishing
a division of Andrews McMeel Universal
1130 Walnut Street, Kansas City, Missouri 64106

www.andrewsmcmeel.com

26 27 28 29 30 VEP 10 9 8 7 6 5 4 3 2 1

Cover design by Leah Meddaoui

Original illustrations by Rupi Kaur
Reimagined illustrations by Leah Meddaoui

ISBN: 979-8-8816-0634-3

Library of Congress Control Number: 2025945680

ATTENTION: SCHOOLS AND BUSINESSES
Andrews McMeel books are available at quantity discounts with bulk purchase for educational, business, or sales promotional use. For information, please email the Andrews McMeel Publishing Special Sales Department: sales@andrewsmcmeel.com.

If you've read any of my poetry, you probably think that I'm very heart-led, and you would be right. Emotions were once my driving force. Whichever direction my heart pointed, I would run without hesitation.

What you may not know is how much that's changed over the years.

When it came to love, being led by my heart came with both rewards and risks. The rewards were exciting, but the risks left me so wounded I lost faith in my heart's ability to guide me. I thought, if I was going to protect myself from heartache, I had to push my heart aside and let my head take the driver's seat. Eventually, I decided it was time I led with reason and logic, rather than feelings.

At first, this new approach seemed to work. I found myself in the kinds of relationships that looked great on paper. The kinds where, after my friends met my partner they gushed, "Oh my god, he's amazing! You're perfect together!"

Yet no matter how amazing they seemed, something always felt off. Rather than listening to my instincts, I stayed in these relationships longer than I should have because I could never put my finger on anything that was actually wrong. Everything looked fine on the outside, so then what was the problem?

Inevitably, we'd break up, and I'd walk away with countless limiting beliefs about love. I began to think all relationships were doomed to fail, and the ones that lasted only did so because people were good at tolerating unhappiness.

When friends fell in love and claimed they had met their person, I asked how they could be so sure. They'd say, "I just *know*," and I'd nod, holding back an eye roll. I didn't believe you could be that sure about anybody.

And then I met him.

It was a day that felt like any other. I spent the morning working through my usual routine. Then that afternoon, I walked into a room that I'll never forget. His back was turned to me when I walked in, but the click-clacking of my heels bouncing off the tiled floor caught his attention. He turned around, our eyes locked, he smiled, and I smiled back.

On any other day, I would've ignored the warm, fuzzy feeling now rising in my belly. I would've diverted my gaze, put more walls up. On many occasions, I had done just that. But that afternoon, my heart threw my head out of the driver's seat and said, "Enough with your rationale, enough with your logic. It's my turn." Completely out of character, I walked over and introduced myself.

Love is like that. Undeniable. Unexplainable. It doesn't knock when it arrives—it walks in like it owns the place. It's not that love is trying to be impolite; it's just that love considers your life its home. And no one knocks on the front door of their own house. Why would love be any different?

By the time he and I finished our first conversation, love had already made itself comfortable in the room of my heart. It was dancing through the halls of my mind. It was redecorating. Painting my thoughts a new color. Wiping down the windows of my eyes to help me see clearly.

Suddenly, I was thinking and doing things I'd never done before, yet I felt more like myself than I had in a long time. Love was altering my DNA. It was Technicolor. Electric. It was pure presence. Love was a rebirth. It made music sound different. Time didn't feel linear anymore—it slowed and stretched.

How had this happened? How long would it last? Was it real? Or was it all in my head? I demanded so many answers from love.

But to uncover love's mysteries would mean having power over it, and having power over love is impossible. It's love that has power over us. To uncover its inner workings would mean love isn't magic, and if there's one thing I now know, it's that love might be the only true magic that exists in this world.

This love reminded me of a poem I wrote years ago:

> they should feel like home
> a place that grounds your life
> where you go to take the day off
>
> - *the one*

Love was a metaphor back then. Now, it is just as that poem described.

Each morning, I turn over to look at the man lying next to me, and the feeling I get when I see him looking back, wearing the same giddy smile I'm wearing, is awe-inspiring. It's my favorite part of the day. I try to find the perfect words to describe this feeling, but no matter what I write, the words fall short. I write anyway; even if it's impossible to capture love, poetry can at least come close.

This book contains my love poems from all my previous collections. I've gathered them here as a celebration of love—its magic, its messiness, its power, and its truth—a reminder to us all that love does exist and that it's always worth fighting for.

i want you to wipe away
everything you know about love
and start with one word
kindness
give it to them
let them give it to you
be two pillars
equal in your love
and you'll carry empires on your backs

the universe took its time on you
crafted you to offer the world
something different from everyone else
when you doubt
how you were created
you doubt an energy greater than us both

- *irreplaceable*

you must
want to spend
the rest of your life
with yourself
first

for the love of my life
i am trying my best to have hope
i'll keep greeting each morning
with an *i will*
when it feels like i can't
i will
i will
i will
meet a day that will melt me
i will move and the sadness *will*
fall off my shoulders
to make room for joy
i will be full of color
i will touch the sky again

no
it won't
be love at
first sight when
we meet it'll be love
at first remembrance cause
i've seen you in my mother's eyes
when she tells me to marry the type
of man i'd want to raise my son to be like

when you start loving someone new
you laugh at the indecisiveness of love
remember when you were sure
the last one was *the one*
and now here you are
redefining *the one* all over again

- a fresh love is a gift

what is stronger
than the human heart
which shatters over and over
and still lives

how you love yourself is
how you teach others
to love you

i will welcome
a partner
who is my equal

you are the faint line
between faith and
blindly waiting

- letter to my future lover

if i'm going to share my life with a partner
it would be foolish not to ask myself
twenty years from now
is this person going to be
someone i still laugh with
or am i just distracted by their charm
do i see us evolving into
new people by the decade
or does the growing ever come to a pause
i don't want to be distracted
by the looks or the money
i want to know if they pull
the best or the worst out of me
deep at the core are our values the same
in thirty years will we still
jump into bed like we're twenty
can i picture us in old age
conquering the world
like we've got young blood
running in our veins

- checklist

love will come
and when love comes
love will hold you
love will call your name
and you will melt
sometimes though
love will hurt you but
love will never mean to
love will play no games
cause love knows life
has been hard enough already

you are a mirror
if you continue to starve yourself of love
you'll only meet people who'll starve you too
if you soak yourself in love
the universe will hand you those
who'll love you too

- a simple math

i'd be lying if i said
you make me speechless
the truth is you make my
tongue so weak it forgets
what language to speak in

my name
sounds so good
french kissing
your tongue

i say maybe this is a mistake.
maybe we need more than love to make this work.

you place your lips on mine.
when our faces are buzzing
with the ecstasy of kissing
you say *tell me that isn't right.*
and as much as i'd like to think with my head.
my racing heart is all that makes sense. there.
right there is the answer you're looking for.
in my loss of breath.
my lack of words.
my silence.
my inability to speak means
you've filled my stomach
with so many butterflies
that even if this is a mistake.
it could only be right
to be this wrong
with you.

i do not need the kind of love
that is draining
i want someone
who energizes me

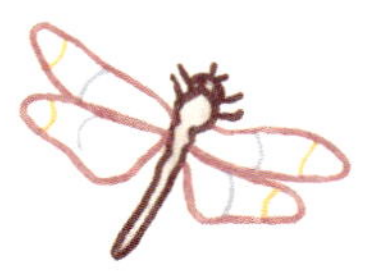

this body was designed to feel and touch. how can i be ashamed of sex. if i was made for. orgasm. after orgasm. with whomever. however. whenever. i choose.

i know i
should crumble
for better reasons
but have you seen
that boy he brings
the sun to its
knees every
night

i do not want to have you
to fill the empty parts of me
i want to be full on my own
i want to be so complete
i could light a whole city
and then
i want to have you
cause the two of us combined
could set it on fire

the orange trees refused to blossom
unless we bloomed first
when we met
they wept tangerines
can't you tell
the earth has waited its whole life for this

- celebration

they should feel like home
a place that grounds your life
where you go to take the day off

- the one

it's easy to love
the nice things about ourselves
but true self-love is
embracing the difficult parts
that live in all of us

- *acceptance*

i could not contain myself any longer
i ran to the ocean
in the middle of the night
and confessed my love for you to the water
as i finished telling her
the salt in her body became sugar

(ode to sobha singh's *sohni mahiwal*)

i need someone
who knows struggle
as well as i do
someone
willing to hold my feet in their lap
on days it is too difficult to stand
the type of person who gives
exactly what i need
before i even know i need it
the type of lover who hears me
even when i do not speak
is the type of understanding
i demand

- the type of lover i need

you must remember it too
how the rest of the city slept
while we sat awakened for the first time
we hadn't touched yet
but we managed to travel in and out
of each other with our words
our limbs dizzying with enough electricity
to form half a sun
we drank nothing that night
but i was intoxicated
i went home and thought
are we soul mates

together we are an endless conversation

to hate
is an easy lazy thing
but to love
takes strength
everyone has
but not all are
willing to practice

you might not have been my first love
but you were the love that made
all the other loves
irrelevant

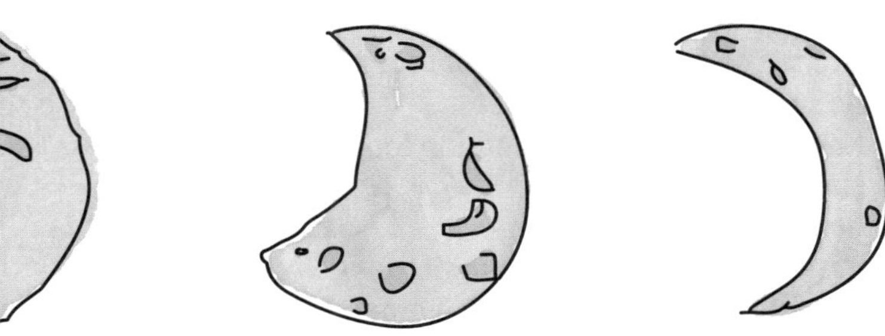

he makes sure to look right at me
as he places his electric fingers on my skin
how does that feel he asks
commanding my attention
responding is out of the question
i quiver with anticipation
excited and terrified for what's to come
he smiles
knows this is what satisfaction looks like
i am a switchboard
he is the circuits
my hips move with his—rhythmic
my voice isn't my own when i moan—it is music
like fingers on a violin string
he sparks enough electricity within me
to power a city
when we finish i look right at him
and tell him
that was magic

this morning
i told the flowers
what i'd do for you
and they blossomed

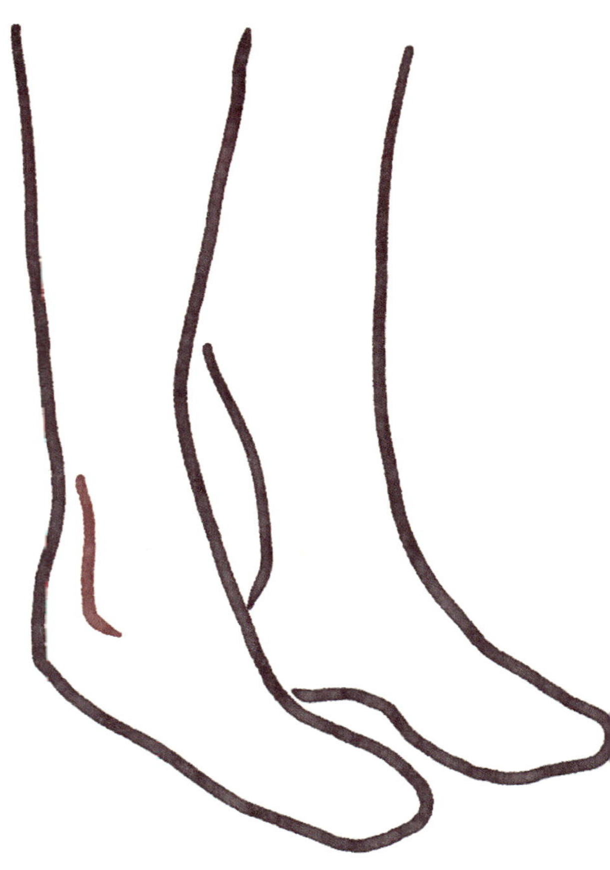

look me in the eyes
when you're down there
eating for your life

- i want you to see what you do to me

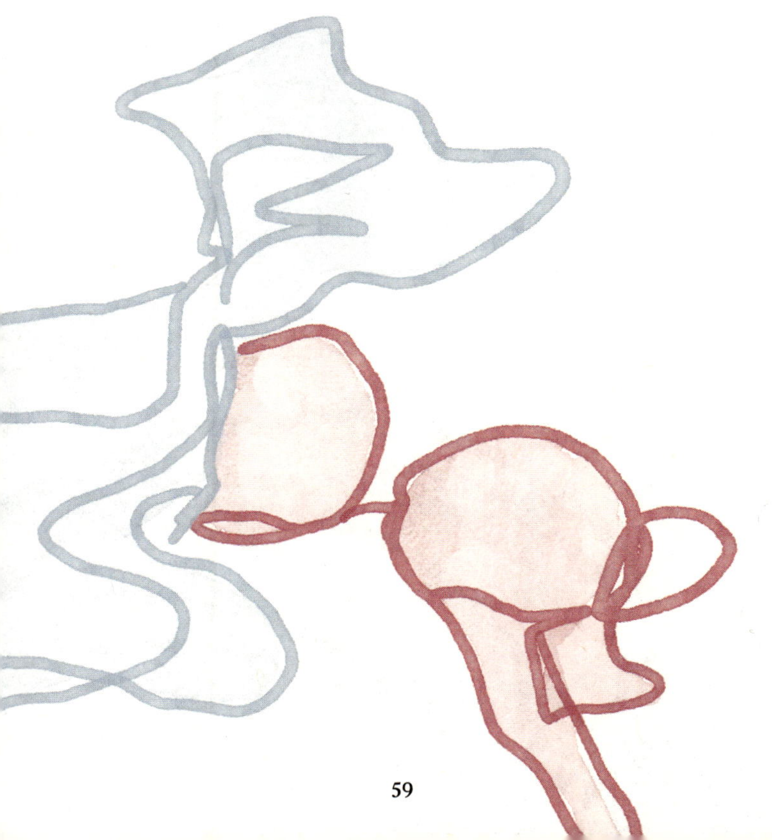

nothing is safer
than the sound of you
reading out loud to me

- the perfect date

how can our love die
if it's written
in these pages

i am trying to not
make you pay for their mistakes
i am trying to teach myself
you are not responsible
for the wound
how can i punish you
for what you have not done
you wear my emotions
like a decorated army vest
you are not cold or
savage or hungry
you are medicinal
you are not them

if you got any more beautiful
the sun would leave its place
and come for you

- the chase

what is it with you and sunflowers he asks

i point to the field of yellow outside
sunflowers worship the sun i tell him
only when it arrives do they rise
when the sun leaves
they bow their heads in mourning
that is what the sun does to those flowers
it's what you do to me

- the sun and her flowers

my favorite thing about you is your smell
you smell like
earth
herbs
gardens
a little more
human than the rest of us

you lose everything
when you don't love yourself

- and gain everything when you do

he placed his hands
on my mind
before reaching
for my waist
my hips
or my lips
he didn't call me
beautiful first
he called me
exquisite

- how he touches me

if i had to walk to get to you
it would take eight hundred and twenty-six hours
on bad days i think about it
what i might do if the apocalypse comes
and the planes stop flying
there is so much time to think
so much empty space wanting to be consumed
but no intimacy around to consume it
it feels like being stuck at a train station
waiting and waiting and waiting
for the one with your name on it
when the moon rises on this coast
but the sun still burns shamelessly on yours
i crumble knowing even our skies are different
we have been together so long
but have we really been together if
your touch has not held me long enough
to imprint itself on my skin
i try my hardest to stay present
but without you here
everything at its best
is only mediocre

- long distance

to be
soft
is
to be
powerful

i am learning
how to love him
by loving myself

what am i to you he asks
i put my hands in his lap
and whisper *you*
are every hope
i've ever had
in human form

i want your hands
to hold
not my hands
your lips
to kiss
not my lips
but other places

for
you
there is still
so much
poetry
in
me

you are a soul. a world. a portal. a spirit.
you are never alone.
you are organs and blood and flesh and muscle.
a colony of miracles weaving into each other.

my body is so hot from wanting you
i'm spilling by the time we take our clothes off
i want the kind of love that
transcends me
into another realm
i want you so deep
we enter the spirit world
go from being gentle to rough
i want eye contact
spread my legs to
opposite ends of the room
and look with your fingers
i want my soul to be touched
by the tip of yours
i want to come
out of this room
different people

- can you do that

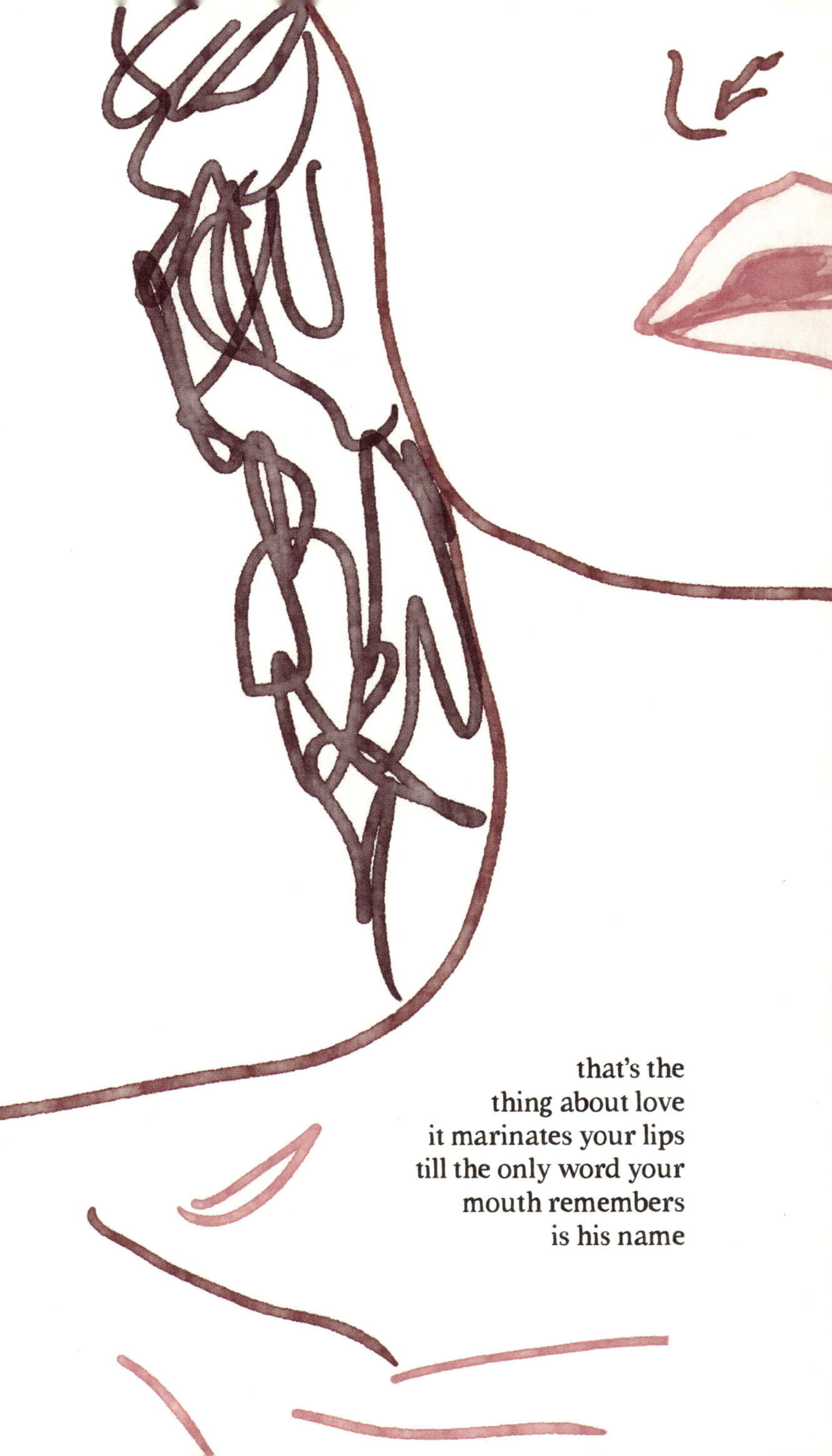

that's the
thing about love
it marinates your lips
till the only word your
mouth remembers
is his name

sometimes
i stop myself from
saying the words out loud
as if leaving my mouth too often
might wear them down

- i love you

poetry is the language of human emotion.
it is air and fire and water and soil.
poetry is the breath in our lungs.
the sighs. the stutters.
poetry is the first time
you fall in love. and it breaks you.
poetry is hunger. the words hanging
in the space between two mouths,
right before the kiss.
the thrill.
poetry is when your stomach
is so heavy with butterflies,
it drops down to your feet.
poetry is the light you walk away with
after digging yourself out of grief.
it is long conversations by the ocean.
poetry is winter's first snowfall.
the smell of cookies in the oven.
poetry is sex. elation.
how we fight and make up.
the journey. the story.
running and laughing. laughing and running.
poetry is the might of one person,
and the echo of billions.
our survival is poetry.
our lives are poetry. and the final act
is writing it down.

the love of family
friends and community
is just as potent
as the love
of a romantic relationship

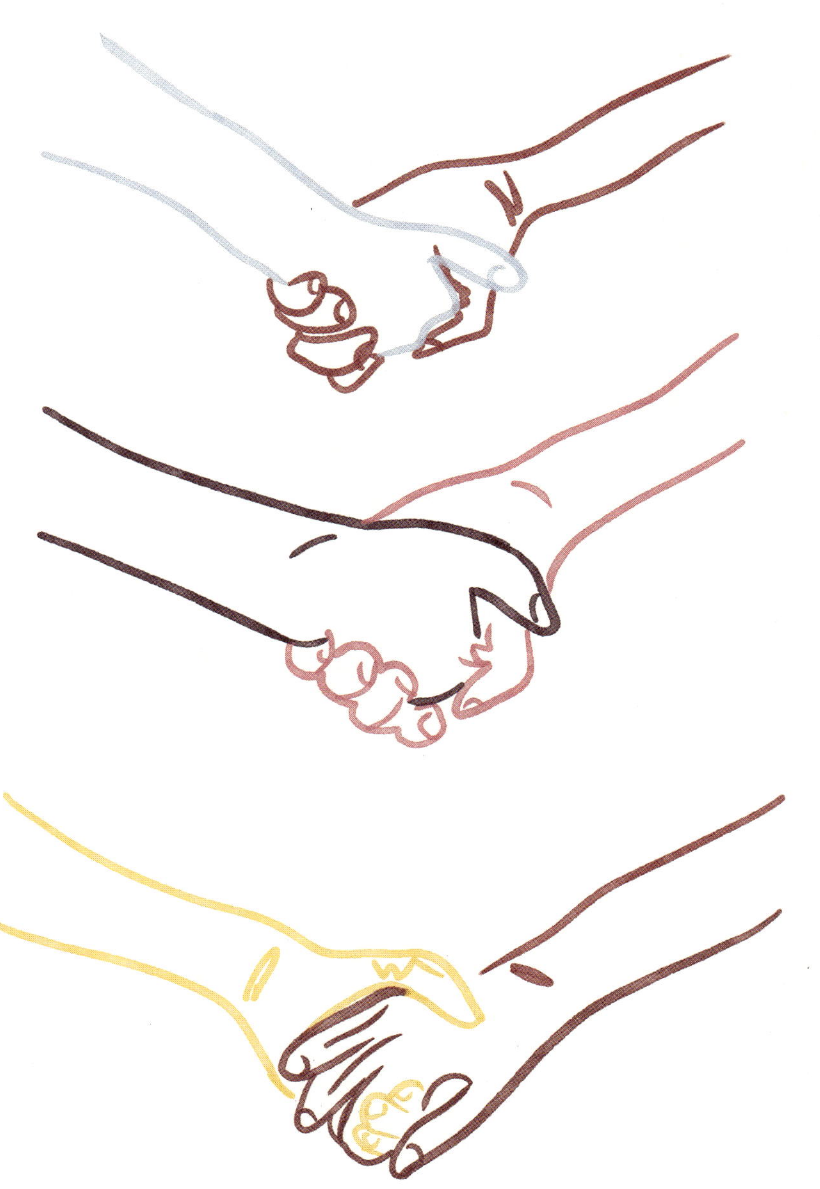

you were desperate for passion
and there i was
the explosion
the freak
the city on fire
what woman could make you feel
more alive than me

i am loving myself out of the dark

we've been arguing more than we ought to. about things neither of us remember or care about cause that's how we avoid the bigger questions. instead of asking why we don't say *i love you* to one another as often as we used to. we fight about things like: who was supposed to get up and turn the lights off first. or who was supposed to pop the frozen pizza in the oven after work. taking hits at the most vulnerable parts of one another. we're like fingers on thorns honey. we know exactly where it hurts.

and everything is on the table tonight. like that one time you whispered a name i'm pretty sure wasn't mine in your sleep. or last week when you said you were working late. so i called work but they said you'd already left a couple hours ago. where were you for those couple hours.

i know. i know. your excuses make all the sense in the world. and i get a little carried away for no good reason and eventually begin crying. but what else do you expect baby. i love you so much. i'm sorry i thought you were lying.

that's when you hold your head with your hands in frustration. half begging me to stop. half tired and sick of it. the toxin in our mouths has burnt holes in our cheeks. we look less alive than we used to. less color in our faces. but don't kid yourself. no matter how bad it gets we both know you still wanna nail me to the ground.

especially when i'm screaming so loud our fighting wakes the neighbors. and they come running to the door to save us. baby don't open it.

instead. lie me down. lay me open like a map. and with your finger trace the places you still want to **** out of me. kiss me like i am the center point of gravity and you are falling into me like my soul is the focal point of yours. and when your mouth is kissing not my mouth but other places. my legs will split apart out of habit. and that's when. i pull you in. welcome you. home.

when the entire street is looking out their windows wondering what all the commotion is. and the fire trucks come rolling in to save us but they can't distinguish whether these flames began with our anger or our passion. i will smile. throw my head back. arch my body like a mountain you want to split in half. baby lick me.

like your mouth has the gift of reading and i'm your favorite book. find your favorite page in the soft spot between my legs and read it carefully. fluently. vividly. don't you dare leave a single word untouched. and i swear my ending will be so good. the last few words will come. running to your mouth. and when you're done. take a seat. cause it's my turn to make music with my knees pressed to the ground.

sweet baby. this. is how we pull language out of one another with the flick of our tongues. this is how we have the conversation. this. is how we make up.

- how we make up

there is no place
i end and you begin
when your body
is in my body
we are one person

- *sex*

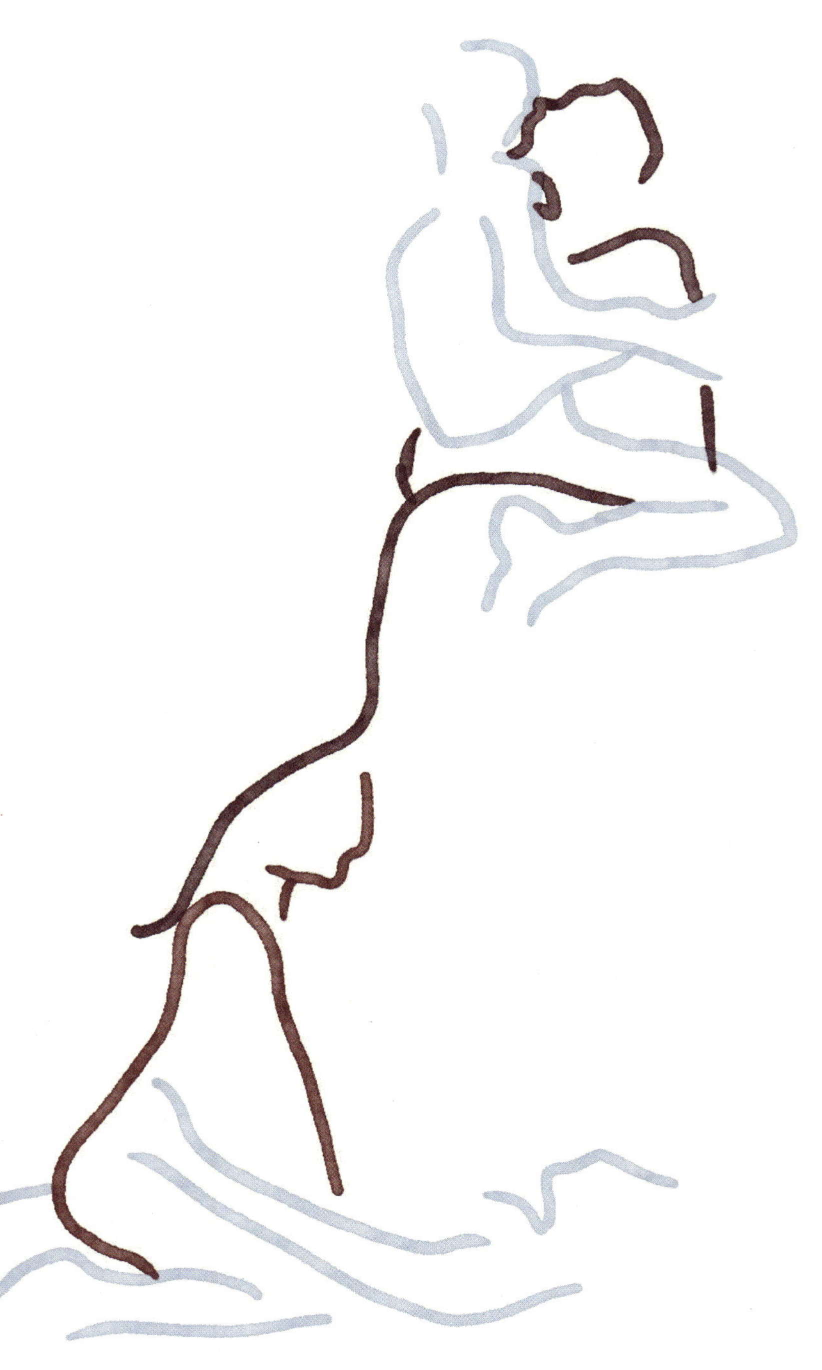

your voice does to me
what autumn does to trees
you call to say hello
and my clothes fall naturally

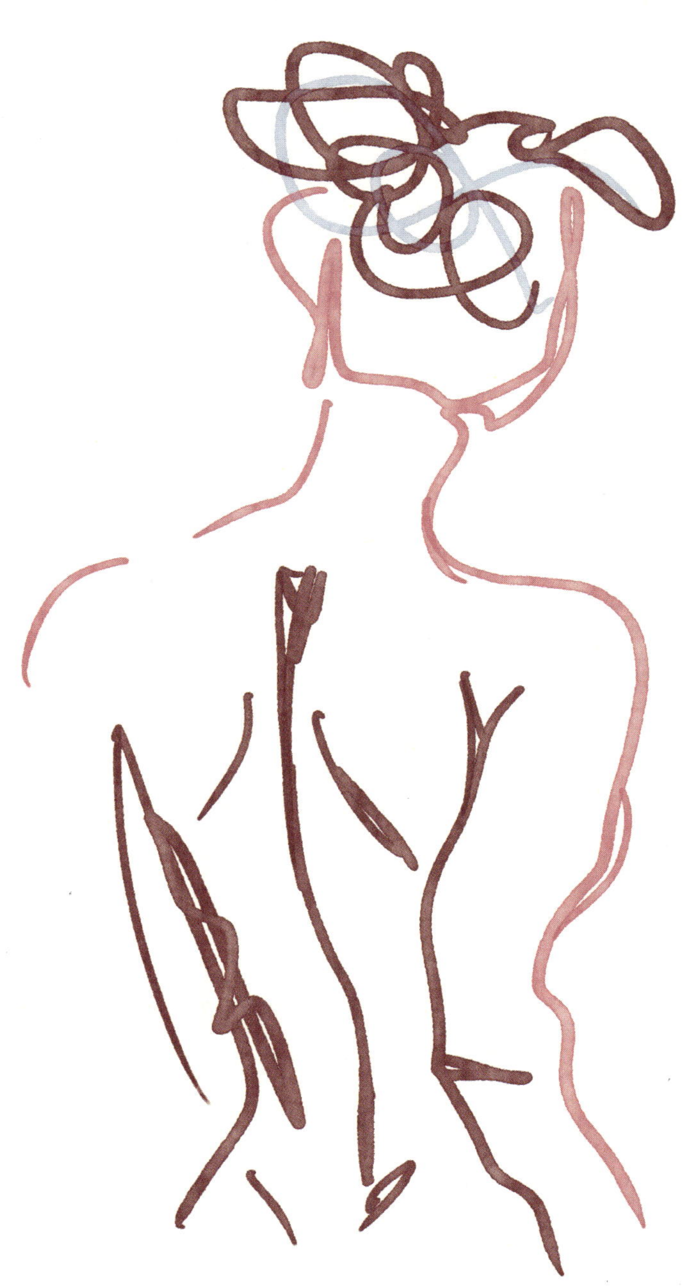

when you are
full
and i am
full
we are two suns

you wrap your fingers
around my hair
and pull
this
is how you make
music out of me

- *foreplay*

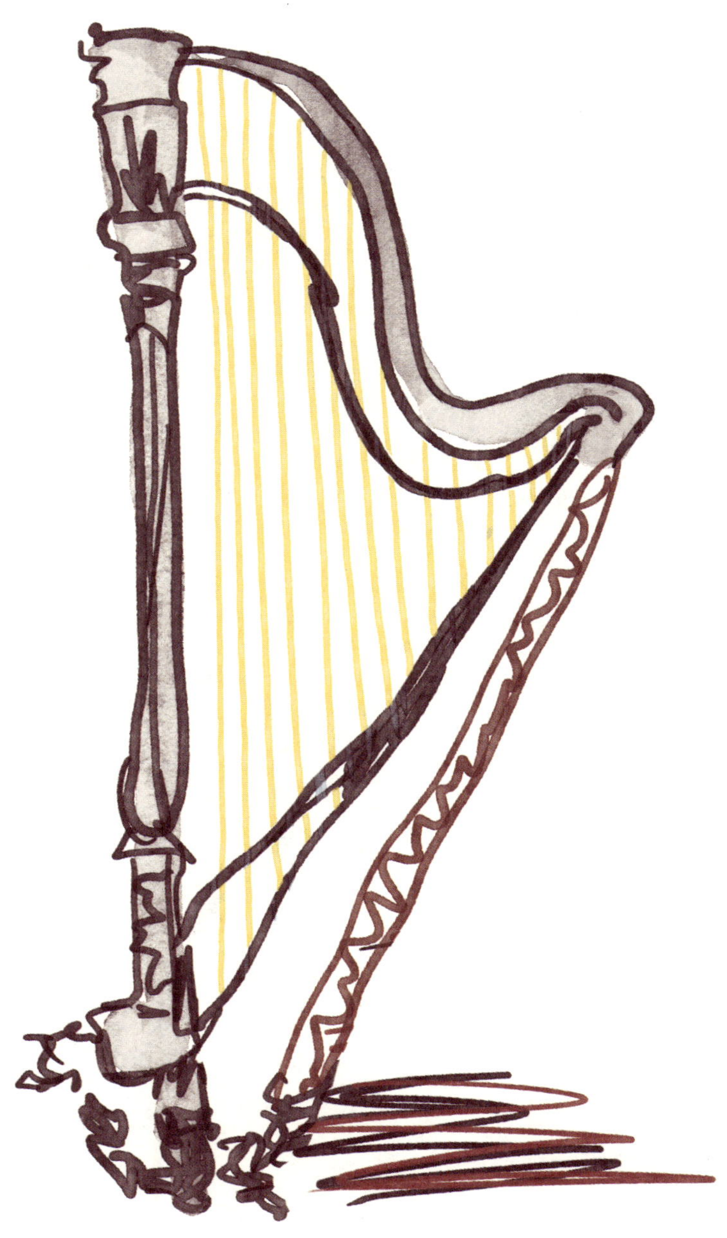

it was as though
someone had slid ice cubes
down the back of my shirt

- orgasm

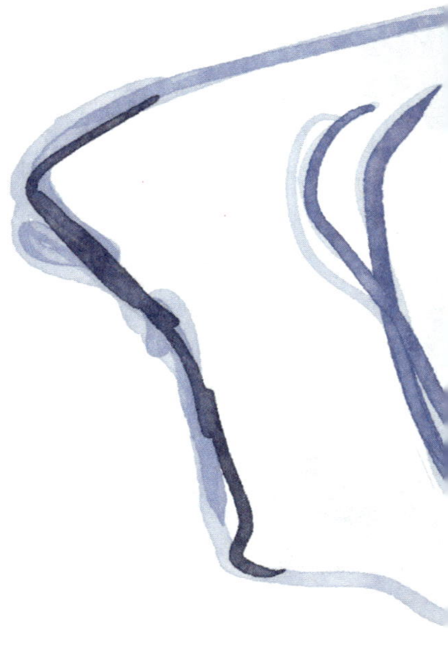

today i saw myself for the first time
when i dusted off
the mirror of my mind
and the woman looking back
took my breath away
who was this beautiful beastling
this extra-celestial earthling
i touched my face and my reflection
touched the woman of my dreams
all her gorgeous smirking back at me
my knees surrendered to the earth
as i wept and sighed at how
i'd gone my whole life
being myself
but not seeing myself
spent decades living inside my body
never left it once
yet managed to miss all its miracles
isn't it funny how you can
occupy a space without
being in touch with it
how it took so long for me
to open the eyes of my eyes
embrace the heart of my heart
kiss the soles of my swollen feet
and hear them whisper
thank you
thank you
thank you
for noticing

give me laugh lines and wrinkles
i want proof of the jokes we shared
engrave the lines into my face like
the roots of a tree that grow deeper
with each passing year
i want sunspots as souvenirs
for the beaches we laid on
i want to look like i was
never afraid to let the world
take me by the hand
and show me what it's made of
i want to leave this place knowing
i did something with my body
other than trying to
make it look perfect

fingers

the most important conversations
we'll have are with our fingers
when yours nervously graze mine
for the first time during dinner

they'll tighten with fear
when you ask to see me again next week
but as soon as i say yes
they'll stretch out in ease

when they grasp one another
while we're beneath the sheets
the two of us will pretend
we're not weak in the knees

when i get angry
they'll pulse with bitter cries
but when they tremble for forgiveness
you'll see what apologies look like

and when one of us is dying
on a hospital bed at eighty-five
your fingers will grip mine
to say things words can't describe

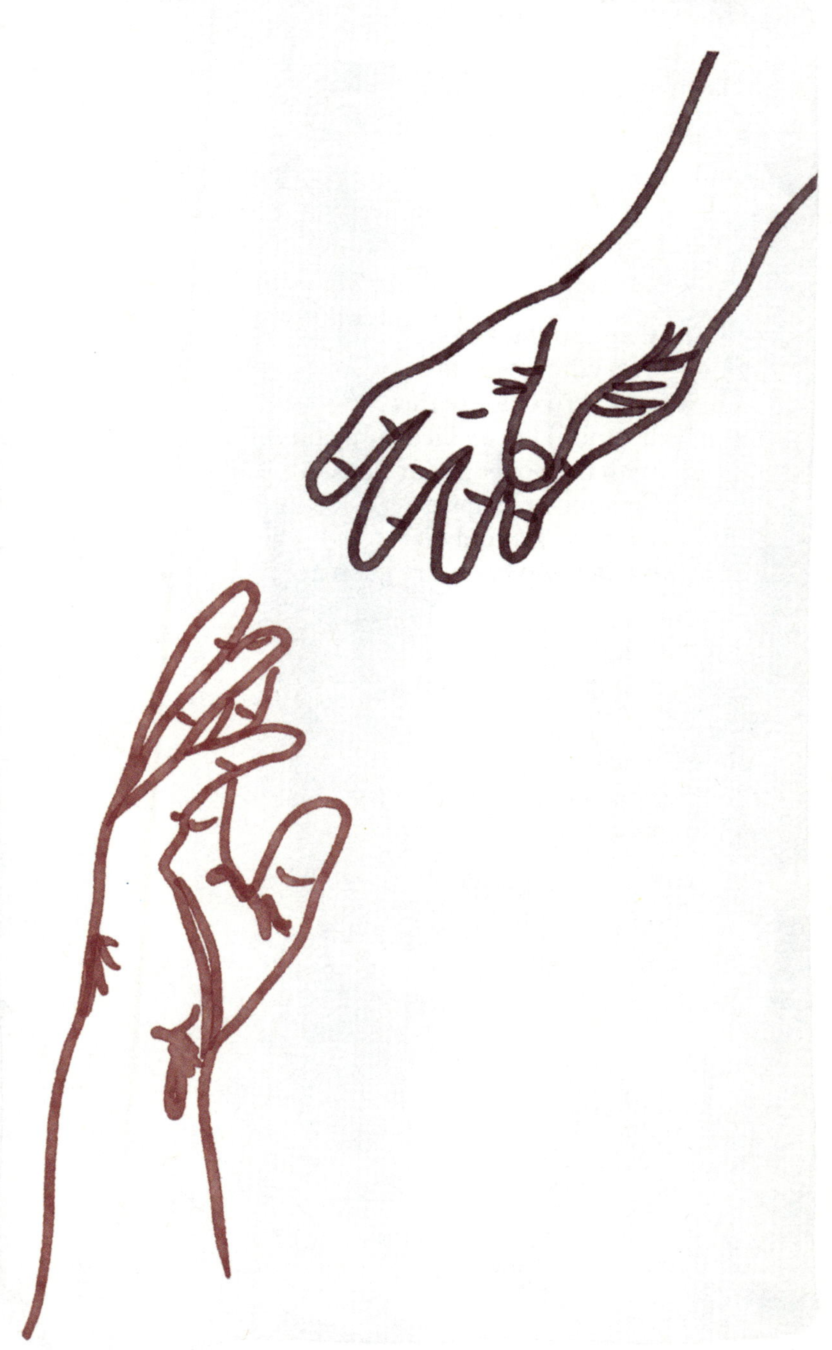

they could take away
everything we have
and we'd conjure this
beautiful life up all over again
with the bones in our backs
building an empire
from the ground up
is exactly what we're good at

when death
takes my hand
i will hold you with the other
and promise to find you
in every lifetime

- commitment

i have
what i have
and i am happy

i've lost
what i've lost
and i am
still
happy

- outlook

make it a point
to love yourself
as fiercely as you do other people

- commitment

god must have kneaded you and i
from the same dough
rolled us out as one on the baking sheet
must have suddenly realized
how unfair it was
to put that much magic in one person
and sadly split that dough in two
how else is it that
when i look in the mirror
i am looking at you
when you breathe
my own lungs fill with air
that we just met but we
have known each other our whole lives
if we were not made as one to begin with

- our souls are mirrors

most importantly love
like it's the only thing you know how
at the end of the day all this
means nothing
this page
where you're sitting
your degree
your job
the money
nothing even matters
except love and human connection
who you loved
and how deeply you loved them
how you touched the people around you
and how much you gave them

Resources

Love Poems by Rupi Kaur is a collection of Rupi's most beloved love poems from across her first five books. If you are inspired to explore more of Rupi's writing, the resource list below notes the book in which each of the poems in this collection originally appeared.

milk and honey, 2015
Pages 4, 8, 14, 18, 22, 26, 29, 36, 38, 46, 52, 60, 61, 68, 72, 76, 80, 82, 83, 89, 100, 101, 108, 122, 128

the sun and her flowers, 2017
Pages 2, 10, 12, 16, 20, 24, 30, 32, 40, 41, 44, 48, 49, 50, 54, 56, 62, 64, 66, 74, 90, 102, 104, 107, 110, 116, 120, 126

home body, 2020
Pages 1, 6, 42, 58, 70, 86, 88, 94, 98, 112, 114, 118, 124

healing through words, 2022
Page 92

milk and honey: 10th Anniversary Collector's Edition, 2024
Pages 34, 84, 96

KEY TO MY HEART

TO:

FROM:

TO:
FROM:

WE
NAILED
THIS
FRIEND-
SHIP

LOVE
YOU'RE MY
FAVORITE
CHAPTER

LOVE YOU WITH
ALL MY BUTT

TO MY
PERFECT
MATCH

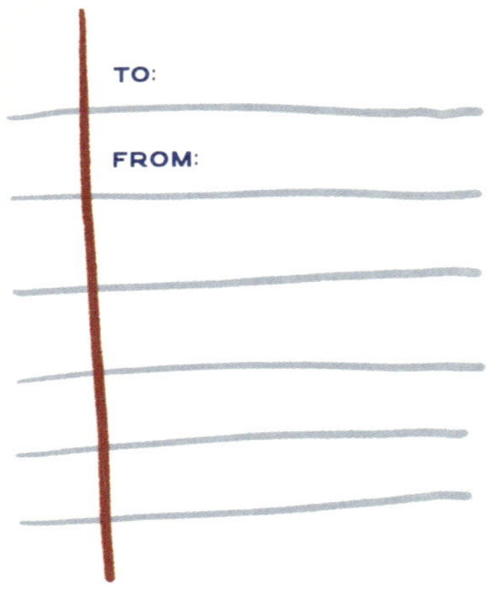

TO:

FROM:

YOU FEEL LIKE HOME

YOU'RE HOT

KISS
XO
BE MINE
I LOVE YOU
HUG
ME+YOU
LOVE
WITH ALL MY HEART(S)

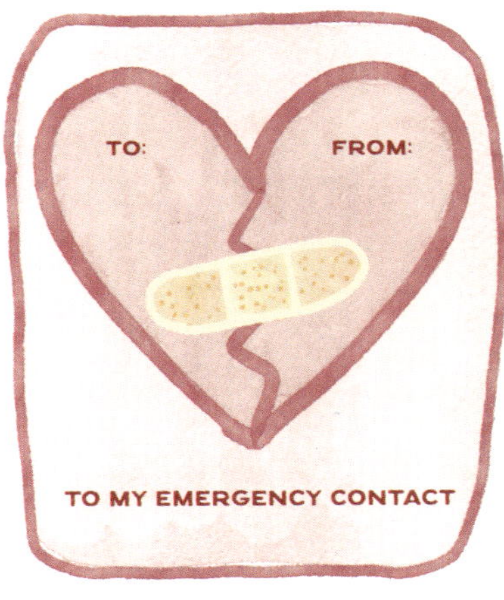
TO:
FROM:
TO MY EMERGENCY CONTACT

BE MY GALENTINE?
TO:
FROM:

TO:

FROM:

TO:

FROM:

TO:

FROM:

SENDING YOU
ALL MY LOVE

TO:

FROM:

TO:

FROM:

YOU ARE MY
SOUL MATE

TO:

FROM:

YOU MAKE MY
HEART SKIP A BEAT